Bonfire of the Verities

Bonfire of the Verities

Michael Lieberman

Texas Review Press
Huntsville, Texas

FIRST EDITION, 2013
Requests for permission to reproduce material from this work should
be sent to:

   Permissions
   Texas Review Press
   English Department
   Sam Houston State University
   Huntsville, TX 77341-2146

Acknowledgements:

"Notes Toward a Theology of Doubt" appeared in an earlier version in
Improbable Worlds, an anthology of Texas and Louisiana Poets, selected
and edited by Martha Serpas, Mutabilis Press, Houston, TX, 2011.

"Defining Depression," "Hospital," "Pittsburgh Writ Large," and
"Remembering Two Teachers" appeared in earlier versions in *Michael
Lieberman: Notes for a Journey, Poems for a Fiftieth Reunion, Shady Side
Academy Class of 1959, 2009*, Privately printed.

"The Color of God's Eyes" first appeared in *The Methodist DeBakey
Cardiovascular Journal.*

To contact Michael Lieberman write to him at: poet@lieberman.net.
To learn more about him and his work visit his website:
www.michaellieberman.com

Library of Congress Cataloging-in-Publication Data

Lieberman, Michael, 1941-
   [Poems. Selections]
   Bonfire of the verities / Michael Lieberman.
      pages ; cm
   ISBN 978-1-937875-30-5 (pbk. : alk. paper)
   I. Title.
   PS3562.I434B66 2013
   811'.54--dc23

                                                     2013013294

For Susan
whose love sustains

and

For our grandchildren
Alexia, Aviva, Casey, Julian, and Zachery

Table of Contents

Bonfire of the Verities

The Color of God's Eyes

Spinoza, God-intoxicated lens grinder,
knows the color of God's eyes, though
he chooses not to say, to cloud the issue
over like a cataract, to force us to contemplate
a face-to-face encounter with the darkness.
When we had our icons it was easier—
we could avert our eyes from his with confidence.
There was a heaven and a hell to burn in,
a place to pasture sheep. Refuge.
Like the patriarchs Spinoza has come
face to face with God. In good conscience
he cannot reveal their color. The brave man
chooses to be cast out and shunned
rather than sow discord with his doubt.
God, he thinks, has no eye, unless
it is the eye of the storm—the one we swirl
and swill in the taverns of our contemplation,
waiting for this Dutch Jacob to return
from his encounter, declare the contest
a draw and tell us that to be released
to life again, he has had to sign
a nondisclosure agreement, that all
he is permitted to say is that God,
who has one evil eye and one good one,
is the moving force of the universe.

Sphinx Moth

A sphinx moth sleeps under a light at the bus terminal.
All dressed up and no place to go.
All dressed up and everyplace to go.
A sphinx moth feeds at the honeysuckle,
sleeps in the night, waits for a call on his cell phone
or someone to come by with a question.
Not much you can't find on an iPhone these days.
One evening a girl does come by.
She tries out a conjecture on the drowsy moth:
The illuminated mysterious is the moth
and the moth is the word
and the word is the raptor
which hunts in the darkness,
solders the sequined light in place,
outlines and decorates the formless surface—
in the end what is fashioned
is only a beginning, as at every instant
of a journey another is beginning.
There are as many journeys as points on a line—
as many lines and lines of thought
as there are points and points of departure.
Look, the moth says, I've spent a lot of time
hanging out at the bus terminal. And sleeping.
You give me too much credit.

Specific Gravity

> The density of a substance
> relative to that of water or air

Specific gravity is not specific,
not at all—at this moment
rosemary grows in our kitchen.
It measures one thing relative
to another—to light or drought
to sun and nutrients, perhaps to love,
or what the final meaning of fragrance is—
and in the bargain assures us
there is no final meaning.

Yet all the while we know
things finally mean—wars mean,
desecrations mean. Every incursion
has a specific gravity at every
check point in every parched land.

Gravity is always specific—
it is June, 1940 and the Germans
are advancing everywhere
and you are nine and running
with your family and escape
to X where they only have food
to feed themselves and you watch
your father swell and starve to death.
Or Hungary in 1956 or Prague Spring,
Arab Spring, Pinochet, the Towers.

(Gettysburg, Leningrad, Dachau—
the list is too long for a poem, a book, a library.)

The moisture of the spirit is relative
like a kiss, like humidity.
The world is full of specific gravities—
your four-year-old has cancer
of both eyes and doctors can save
his life but not his sight.
Your mother's Alzheimer's disease
that is yours as well as hers.

Earth has specific gravity, fire does.
Together they might be a consuming,
inelastic darkness—or a shelter.
Gravity is always specific as when
you get laid off in Detroit when your line
closes and your benefits run out,
and you are fifty-seven in January
with no heat. No one needs janitors
to sweep up broken glass and the leaves
the bitter wind pushes through the windows.

The number of specific gravities
in each heart grows at every second,
expands faster than the universe—
the specific gravity of connection,
of dissolution. Of stone or dust.
How many specific gravities of love
can we count—or grief or loss?
Tears have a specific gravity of one
against which everything else is measured.

The universe expands, our lives
drift, children learn to count
and what they can count on.
Conjecture joins things together,
sometimes absurdly, sometimes not.

You can almost be sure all gravity
is specific until the final freezing
of water in our landscape.

The Reason for Flowers

Each fall in Houston I'm bullish on flowers.
I never sell them short. I hunt bargains
like a Wall Street trader, values with an upside
that will shine in the winter darkness,
sound stock with growth potential,
impervious to cranky winds and intrusive frosts.
In a down market traders hedge.
I pass on Transvaal daisies.
Petunias will fade like a floozy at a truck stop.
I'll earn a little profit with begonias,
take a mild risk with impatiens.
In my yard, which swings hysterically between sun and shade,
I'll place a bet on sweet alyssum,
nothing elaborate, just a few pots
in the sun next to the warmth of the house.
Some dark morning three months hence
I'll get down on my knees, push my snoot
into those pots and breathe in the deep feminine—
which is the only reason for flowers.

Notes Towards a Theology of Doubt

1.

"Trust in God and keep your powder dry"
is a Cromwell quote we might apply
in place of *Fide Semper Vincere*.
I'll raise a glass of cold Vouvray
or a Bud or mug of Guinness Stout
to all of those who favor doubt.
I count myself among the pack
that sees faith riding on doubt's back.

2.

In the event of my death
remember it is timely.
Who can live, abundantly
or otherwise, beyond
what neutral circumstance permits?

3.

A torrential rain off the Gulf
has puddled in my driveway.
Mare nostrum, I remember—
the Romans owned it all, or everything
they thought worth owning. I am,
I think, master of a disappearing pond.

4.

I am one who ignores
advice and could succumb
to gluttony if the Lord
would grant me petit fours,
but if he plays the maverick
and offers up Italian—
sweet Lord, think linguine with clams—
I'll be pleased to suffer garlic.

5.

I am death's customer,
sure I want to purchase nothing
in his kiosk of rancid wares—
I ask for a store credit, I tell him
I'll wait for the new lines in the spring.

6.

What would you say to a wager—
a bet that somewhere between
Whole Foods and Krogers
there are the hungry and the needy
and I am going to pass them by?

7.

Sun going down on Memorial Day,
and through the chain link fence—
oleander, the burl of a long dead

tree stuck in the links, persisting
like gristle between the teeth.

8.

Some days I walk flat-footed,
sometimes I shuffle or shamble,
or gimp—disguise my arrival,
hoping death will bar the door
and turn the bolt against my entry.

9.

Received wisdom at a gas station
on the card of a real estate broker—
Isaiah 32:18: And my people
shall dwell in a peaceable habitation.
Omitted are the street address and zip code.

10.

All roads lead to Rome
except the Tour de France
except the Ringstrasse,
that Ouroboros of faded modernity,
except the bridge to Toledo
except the Trail of Tears
except the road to Santiago de Compostela
except the autostrada to Firenze
from Rome which leads
like the others to our eking out
the yardage of our forward progress.

11.

A solitary wasp ignores
the blossoms of my vinca
and forages beneath the leaves.
What can her quest be
that commands my full attention?

12.

I must manage with the quotidian,
never accepting less, never waiting
at the bus stop of a shabby barrio
or in imagined savannas and open forests—
waiting for fineness to crystallize
into my life, never accepting imperatives.

13.

Who has agency in the hardscrabble
land of the spirit, unless it is
our impoverished selves, famished,
each of us, feral and lost,
in the iPhone marshes of the present?

14.

Civility in all things civil
is what we need, Jung thought.
Yet consider an assault on darkness,
the high barricade to be breached
with total disregard for form if we are
to return to a common discourse for our woes.

15.

I'll not disguise my lewdness
when it comes to flowers.
Earlier you glimpsed forsythia,
which makes me randy, crazy with lust.
Now I offer you six newly planted roses,
every thorn starved for water
in the inferno of a Houston summer.

16.

We live under the freeway of ourselves,
our urban shades our meager offering,
illuminated by trafficking in the only
squalid splendor we can know.

Presence

The hydrangea sits
a single clot
along the edge
of the fence
my neighbor's dogs
have chewed
and burrowed under.
Not the least perturbed
a single globe
a world with an end
a two-week lease
perfect in its time.

In This Poem I Predict the Coming of the Messiah

Set aside from each other like birch
and olive tree are the "I"s and "thou"s
that steal each other's lines
in a bad comedy skit. Who says,
Many are called and few are chosen, or
Called or not the gods are present?
We are the Torquemadas of ourselves—
who else can we be? We are
called out, found out by our torments.
What if one's calling
is not to come out but to wind
around the stylus of one's self,
spindled and waiting
to wring small miracles of doubt
from the latrine within?
Or to unwind, to wend toward
a black province after the sun
drops dead and mosquitoes suck
you dry of everything but
the pure discomfort of being?
Now you're talking Messiah.
(Don't think those uninvited gods
don't have their own problems
with gout and vermin. You are
not alone in gratitude for
strong coffee and the sunrise.)
To be self-piked, self-impaled
by one's innards, is unbearable.
A god has to do what a god has to do.
You wait in a dark cave for three days,

hoping the mystery will swaddle you,
the transcendent other will suffuse you,
and then you get the fuck out
before the roof caves in.

Medical Emergency

Cardiac tamponade whittles you down
to a nub of pencil. Withers you.
You set the pencil down and rest.
Your heartbeat so faint you cannot
mark even an X to any decent act,
your murmurs of ascent inaudible,
your doubts muffled beyond sonar.
The python within squeezes you—
you hesitate without missing a beat.
Oxygen waits in your lungs for an entry visa.
The flow of lymph is more than you
can manage. I tell you with all my heart—
Cardiac tamponade is the black death of our time.

Laser Bearer

Star bound
earth bound
you festoon
the path
with punctate
darkness

Once I thought
to penetrate
the dured
evanescence—
I could not
unless I
entered through
such fenestrations—
and only
for an instant

That flash
blinded me
exposed
the neural lapse—
that enduring gap
hard-wired
always present
in the vagabond
heart
the cribriform
heart
the troubadour
heart

The Cloisters

We took the A train as instructed.
Of course they were old instructions,
and whatever it was he wanted us to do
in Harlem, we didn't. We had other plans
that morning, though by mistake
we got off at a hundred and ninth to ask.
Oh, you're way too early. Catch the next one
north—which is what we did.
Okay, I thought, this is okay
as we rattled amidst noise and sway
and determined Kindle readers.
I tried to imagine the way it was
for Trappist monks during the long,
silent winters of Northern France—
only the chanting and the wind
and the hope of God's voice.
I admit to guilt around the subject
of extreme submission. Such repose
for me is too much of a good thing.
Sometimes I need to escape the quiet,
though the subway felt like subjugation,
each of us trapped in jarring isolation.
I had no hope of losing myself like the man
across the car who squinted at a Bible.
I was glad when we left the racket and broke
out to the light—the Hudson far below,
still, on a windless day. A brief walk,
and once inside the gates, we faced a swell
of granite, bare and cleft, and everywhere
quarried through with pools of azaleas
and tulips that took us prisoner.

Tuesday Afternoon

In Memory of Jack Gilbert

We don't say much about him,
she smoking a cigarette and I
drinking black coffee from a mug,
both of us looking out on
the street below. Yet something
must be said. He can no longer
speak for himself. Tau protein
has tangled his thought and
plaques have destroyed his words.
Should we mention the girl
in the blue halter below,
or the tree busy being green?
Would that do it, bring back
the Aegean, the black sands
of Santorini or Thira
before the catastrophe—
or him before the slow devastation,
before he was left alone
in the ebb of his thoughts?

Grant's Atlas of Anatomy

My mother lived on fissured hills of fail,
a crumbling landscape I cannot guess,
on denuded ridges almost devoid of gods.
Then Eris in a final act of leaving eroded
her life to a moonscape of despair.
Strange animals rooted in that grave-shale,
unparsible in their ordinary foraging.
I am certain once she was young and lithe,
but later if she danced, she danced alone
in those uncharted regions. Wild
does not describe that strangeness.
Then even the pilot light of her luster
was snuffed out, first turned down
by my father and later doused by booze
and loneliness. The girl in her burned
out long ago. I was blinded by the gloom—
in the fog-bound valleys I could not see
beyond the trailhead. I supposed I knew
the contour of her life from the detailed
map of gyri and sulci I had before me.
For too long I did not know that she was lost
among the ravaged proteins and exploded
vessels or imagine that an evil wind
had blown her out of her life into an abyss.
It is a sadness that before she died
I did not grasp her aloofness was coerced.

Narcissus, the Flower, and Then Some

The light off the sea is erratic
as it tacks across the surface,
subject to the whims of wind and current—
even Apollo is buffeted, lives
the helter-skelter life we all do
as he struggles to catch up,
install a more stable operating system
on his laptop for his traverse.
Enter Narcissus, the flower,
profuse behind a picket fence,
sequestered in a nearby yard—
he has no truck with failed delivery,
disdains incompetence which cannot plan ahead,
looks away like an untargeted missile
with no eye to the sun, no way—
no interest even—in tracking
that sun's arc. He locks in
on one of his stellate blossoms.
The blinding fragrance intoxicates us.
Now even the blind shall see.
We are prisoners of this tyranny,
captives of a warlock in white robes
(well-doused with cheap cologne)—
a klansman, who lures us away from the light.
Narcissus is a solar system of his own.
You cannot blindside this fellow,
he is the star of his own firmament—
the warder of his own presidio.

Found Poem

Some say poems are from God,
the Ghostwriter in the sky,
that

> Frankie Lane
> Lois Lane
> Bowling Lane

are a found poem.

Do not retrieve the triplets.
Leave them in the Lost and Found.
They are foundlings,
fingerlings spawned by neural detritus,
best left orphans.

Let the furies ride in
        and reclaim Frankie Lane.
Let Superman swoop down
        and ravish Lois Lane.
Let the owner of Lanes
        strike fear in us
        and spare us.

Timeless Treasures

After the name of a watch repair shop
La Jolla, California

My friend Igor says it can't be fixed,
the handsome Seiko with its quartz mechanism.
The clock sits mute among my books,
unable to mouth regrets or mutter its curses.
Its frozen innards remember only six-ten—
evening or morning, I wonder.
There are no parts, he tells me.
I try to figure in what year
and in what house technology failed.
It was a gift from another life
now closed off, as distant as the Bulova
and Helbros watches my father sold in Pittsburgh,
as my grandfather's pocket watch denied me
forty years ago by a righteous uncle,
his meanness straight from Faulkner.
Memory does not stop when the movement fails.
Yet the past is occluded—
time lisps imperfectly when it speaks at all.
The only certainties are the Seiko's fine Roman face
and its deliberate hands—a compelling beauty
that records what is lost and found in losing.

An Orange Tree in Autumn
Houston, Texas

This one stands well-sheltered north and west,
the oranges ripening slowly. Like poems
they survive in sundry pockets, in the corners
of yards, unattended, havened by rent houses,
tumble-downs and our own—not quite abandoned,
but feral, without intent, unruly intruders
in our landscape, each a miraculous thicket of promise
left fallow not by truancy or neglect
but by an incremental awareness that awards us being.

Bonfire of the Verities

It his here I heap
the platitudes
I cannot keep

a pyre of pride
ineptitudes
I cannot abide

ideas crustily held
flaky and half-baked—

purity of body and soul
all of it the whole

my sins my good works
dry tinder

a vision of world peace
gets heaped on too

and God a failed
compression algorithm

fawning courtesy
false witness to the self

the belief this flame
is a purifying light

toss on my vaulted glorious ego
to which my self plays gigolo

and heave to these insipid brays
that weigh down my days—

the meek (or strong)
shall inherit the earth

a world without end
is a means to life

dogma and the doctrinaire
can vanquish true despair

the byline of the good
exposes the author of the lie

empirical truth
shall set me free

the ephemeral
will be a light to me

mysticism
will lead me from the mist

everything including
nothing is written down

that this journal entry
is my witness

my animate self inspires
and breathes beyond desires

truth will burn like brush
luminous robust.

This fire burns in me—
it cannot set me free
it leaves me ash, not tree.

Night Fog with Tetanus Shots

The fog hangs on everything—
a loincloth on the scabbard trees,
plastic garbage cans, the broken curb.
A perverse cover up, especially
at night when it invades the house
of the goddess and blinds her
with its matte gray finish.
The night fog has put out the eyes
of Athena. The wanton spills over
its banks and into our lives.
Under its cover Eros lovingly sinks
his fangs into every human neck
and injects his venom.
The wind is spastic, as if paralyzed
by MS. It has a venereal disease
that leads to blindness like syphilis.
The gray-eyed goddess must feel her way
forward, uncurl the fingers of the dead
from the switch, throw it to illuminate
the day. She administers tetanus shots
against the wounds of Eros and rubs
his mordant powder from us with bare hands.
At dawn she puts Aphrodite
and her foul smells to the road,
reaches out to Eros and grabs him
by the balls before he can gouge
her eyes. Later the sun will speckle livid
and set. The night will invite the fog.

X in Winter

Some mornings in the dark corners
of yards in California the tiny
flowers open on the jade plants
and push aside their succulence.
Shelter me. I ignore wisteria today,
their hanging gardens of Babylon.
There is no communing with rosemary,
its ripe smell, its sapphire
emerging ahead of spring.
If you can spare the time away, set
aside the jostle of the everyday
and shelter me. You have no lushness
to unfold—each fleck of petal smaller
and less bold than the marring white fly
that will soon emerge and suck hibiscus dry.
Bougainvillea is a privileged harlot,
a tawdry, difficult, thorny bitch—but comely.
You sit alone on a ledge in a pot,
assimilating minerals and metabolizing
as if the wizardry of the commonplace
were nothing, a nod to the ordinary.
You are a presence inured to every
other event but being. Shelter me.

Conduit

I should not be surprised,
given the folly of rapture
on an ordinary morning like today,
that no one has come, the only
emissary the path itself covered
with well-worn bark and chips
fresh from a storm-downed beech
past the school to the playground.
Yet in that park I had hoped
to look down a length of pipe
into a promissory breech
and see my mother there, young,
as she was when my father
married her or when she suckled me.
A conduit—something concrete,
like those that enchant our children
or guide spent runoff to the sea—
might carry my mother back to me.
Only a fool petitioner would ask
a song or goddess—something rare—
to touch her body and guide it up
or imagine that she, ten years
dead, might climb out to me.
The choice instead must be to put
aside the fear, no, dread, and clamber
down love's trace to enter into her,
who, when I will allow, still suckles me
across this ancient space.

Certain Measures

I am the court Jew of my life,
the guest worker of my soul—
before the gods peck my liver out,
may I convert my truths to doubt.

Vigil

Houston Hospice
September 23, 2010

Hers is an ordinary life that cannot see
the gold amaryllis clinging to bloom
beyond the breezeway, a life no longer hydrated
by the rattle of tubes and lines, the ratchety
click of perverse machines that meter out
hope before a cracking dike. Soon death
will come up over the bayou and swamp her
with no promise of redemption,
no restitution for our loss—
as it is with ordinary lives.
One by one her synapses uncouple
leaving islands of sensate loss,
her dendrites retreat to the shoals,
and she is left adrift in the murk.
Last week, her face, a defiant rictus,
stared down the rising water.
Her eyes closed and the welling-up slid down.
I don't know—no one can see
into the souls of our ordinary lives
as we wait with her for death
to fledge up out of the bayou.
We urge you, make haste, she has slid
past outrage and fear. She waits. We wait.
May the force that animates the waters
draw them up soon and exert a healing tug.
Sweet undertow, our ordinary lives are ready.

Special Commendation
In Memoriam Ruth Abel Perrin
September 24, 2010

Survival was within the bundled shroud
that waits for the fire. Here is the afterlife
of cremation that is sure and certain:
They slip what was Ruth
into a crypt backed by a rectangle
of flame that seems neither hungry
nor ready nor indifferent—
only necessary in the way gravity
is felt even when we are unaware.
Fire is the wordless commendation.
We imagine the water released
early into the stifle of Houston,
a gesture essential and absurd
in the dense humidity of our city.
Then the methane and oxygen
burn through the fat and muscle,
the organs and tissues.
Shorn free by chemistry,
the nitrogen hisses out—
some to be fixed by legumes, the rest,
its oxides, as greenhouse gases.
The carbon dioxide will be
repatriated by the ash trees and elms
that mourn the effaced shtetl of her parents,
by the oaks and black locusts
in the vacant lots of her girlhood Monongahela,
and, too, beyond her body's cinnabar,
by the crimson seeds of magnolia
that mark our neighborhood.
The rest is left to us—

crusts of calcium salts to scatter,
trace metals that will be untraceable.
We commend rare earths to the earth.
This is the death. This is the life.

Giacometti's Armature

Last day of the year
the fog has lifted
like a woman's skirt
revealing
her unshaved legs.
I wait for the sun
to dissolve this metaphor,
a view of the world,
I am unhappy to admit
as mine, admit
to this poem. Edgy,
addicted to radiance,
I want to edit out
the bland, the terrifying,
the black-dog presence,
write a comedy—
foxglove in the open woods,
lawns ending in hydrangea—
hide away burn victims,
those immolated by conviction,
exile fatigue, loneliness,
every affliction,
even lack of
concentration.
This poem
bears the shape
of Giacometti,
who accepted
the ugly
made it
serve beauty—

Giacometti,
whose
armatures
lance
pre-
ten-
sion,
en-
vy.

It's a Matter of Dispute

after a poem by Tess Gallagher

It was bound to happen
that someone would write a poem
about the tallest men in Europe
and publish it in *The New Yorker*
before I got around to writing mine
which in any event has nothing
to do with Montenegro but harks
back to Dante who thought they
came from Friesland which they
may have and the cold wind off
the Waddenzee that June many years ago
when we ate eel and drank old jenever.

Souvenir of Provence

In the square at Gordes
the names cry out for reading.
Time has warped our memories
of the citizens and soldiers who died
in the world wars. They call
from the sewer of history—
the trenches, the gas and typhus,
the disembowelments, all those
who died alone in the mud,
which is to say most, ignored
or forgotten, present this afternoon
on the monument at Gordes.
The names go unnoticed. Perhaps
the light is too fierce for our gaze,
or life's needs too pressing.
Save one fished from the cloacal stream.
Joseph Bonfils died the granite
tells us "in occupation," a sprig
of Sephardic Jewry in the sun,
blooming in the rock, remembered
but unrecognized, a life struggling
to be known in the chaos
of our everyday concerns.
Who is the righteous one
who helped us siphon back
his name from the camps
and brought him to this moment?

A Dark Radiance

My former colleagues melt away in the glare
of reflection. Focus too much light
and the parabola will vaporize the soul.
They have become unrecognizable threads
in an old tapestry I cannot reweave,
brightly colored elemental bits that one day
I again may nest with. Smaller and smaller,
figures fade in the dust of the unswept streets.
Their faces lost in the billowing, I turn the corner.
At autopsy all parts are returned to the body,
slightly molested, minimally rearranged.
Something will fly up when it is ready,
take color from the sun and fall back
beneath the earth in a dark radiance.
I am caught, an oscillating harmonic,
not wanting to be inflected in either direction,
craving above all the infinite antipodes of this finite earth.

Isobars

Houston, Texas
Summer, 2011

There are no texts to consult,
no secret plan or incantation,
only the small green watering can
and the jasmine brown as wrapping paper,
deracinated in the crumbling dirt.
That's what drought is about—
we fight to return the world
to its nature, its roots.
Isobars of high pressure are
perversions we cannot answer,
reprisals from Leviticus
for uncommitted blasphemies.
What this world needs is a drink.
A prophet's anvil to beat
these stinting isobars to wet bars
and quench the delirium
that has settled on this city
and smothers our daily lives.
At this moment, driving home
from work or feeding the kids,
five million parched souls,
bleary with murderous intent,
listen to the weather. They plot
to concoct solutions of their own.

In the Country of Doubt

The coordinates of the country of doubt
are 29°, 45' N / 95°, 21' W.
Here in the fall the cottonwoods
quit at yellow and refuse the red.
In the country of doubt
the future is a clotted gray crystal ball.
Even inert gases have a backup plan.
Squalls from the tropics bring
the bayous over their banks,
yet there is always a drought.
In the coffee shops frappuccino
is the *nom de guerre* of failed ventures.
The poetry slam is subsidence in ascension.
Assertion is retreat.
Film noir is the work of personable extroverts.
Magical realism is unreal.
Somewhere in Harris County
a blacksmith is trying to fit
five hundred horses under
the hood of a Chevy Volt.
In the country of doubt surgeons
pause before the first cut.
Do not resuscitate orders are essential.
Megachurches mime their messages
and Halloween is without costumes.
Savings accounts are empty
and no one wires money
to their relatives in Michoacán.
Sausage makers hedge their bets
and the number of ingredients
unwinds into the hundreds.
New rules for the Astros—
five strikes and you're out.

Everyone is sure and certain
or certain to be sure
or sure of nothing
or sure there is nothing
to be certain about—
surely it is one of these,
although one can't be sure.
Allowing for a margin for error,
old glory has fifty-five stars.
V8s have nine cylinders.
My heart has three ventricles.
The trinity is four—an understudy
is always in the wings.
People question if the Holy Spirit
is wholly a spirit or partially
colored stucco or papier mache.
The pure spirit is purely a spirit.
Polyphemus has binocular vision.
Odysseus is lascivious and mounts a sheep.
Country and Western songs
are enclosed within Austin's City Limits.
People look down that lonesome road
and see a multitude.
As for God, for God's sake,
let's leave him or her or it
or all three out of this.
Even on sunny days
I back this poem up
in the cloud—and
on a second hard drive,
on a thumb drive
and in my email account.
Only one thing's certain here—
doubt is 100% corrosion resistant.

Monterrey Journal
June 14, 2011

Seguridad is what *El Norte*
calls a section of the local news,
which to the people of this city
is as essential as the football scores.
(In this family poem, I leave out
the beheadings, torture, dismem-
berments and hangings, the disappeared
and fire bombings printed there.)
This morning we landed and taxied
past a stealth gray 737, a sheriff's star
emblazoned on the tail and "Federal Police"
across the fuselage. This evening
after work, I spotted seven
armored personnel carriers
marked "Police" bivouacked
in the courtyard of my hotel.
Sometimes I worry, but not tonight.
Seguro is how I feel with all
this firepower at my window,
more than safe, snug, in fact,
in my little air-conditioned prison,
my *cárcelito*—my hovel of
good fortune, of unearned grace.

Pulsatile

Circe is not circadian,
she is the ever-present—
always on the prowl—
born even before the gods
invented systole and diastole,
a pulseless heartthrob
who turns men to steers
and then to grief
with her blowsy ways.
Her wares are the come-on
of Prosecco and roses,
the come down
of roaches and fleas.
You invite yourself in
and she puts out your lights.
You find yourself in the trough
of a featureless landscape
where time is a fog,
each day a day in November,
stripped to your skivvies
in the muck with the others,
dimly aware of your nowhere.
(Here, sports scores don't matter,
you forgo the cheap booze
and the chips, the breath mints,
the latest news of the market.)
You are a castrated gladiator,
too weak to raise a sword.
What you retain is your hate
for your slough-mates
who vie for her hand.
You are sure she will return,
choose you alone,

ungeld you, make a man of you,
anoint you her consort.
Oh, how you long to be chattel,
a homunculus of the self
you were and nothing more.
You are not man enough
to know what to wish for—
the intervention of a god,
a Poseidon, a Zeus or a Thor,
a shave and a ferry ticket
across the still waters,
safe conduct to your own heartbeat,
the restoring balm of violent storms,
their bracing peaks and disheartening troughs.

In Praise of the Arts

Ein bisschen Titian
kindles frisson.

For My Father

after A.Z.

He scattered them through his book
like pebbles in the woods, hoping
somehow to find his way back
to the trails they hiked together,
poems that his father will not see,
poems of the living disappeared.
My poems for my father
are poems of the dead disappeared,
gone thirty-five years, recalled
imprecisely like morning sun
filtered through a spider's web
that catches the light but does not hold it,
drops of adhered moisture
refracting the light, not focusing it.
That's how precision works—
fifty approximations and you have
something that is not your father,
not the way he held you
when you were small
but a constellated presence.
That is what memory gives us,
a stand-in, a grotesque understudy,
caught in a threadbare web,
sagging under the weight
of beaded particulate absence.

Remembering My Mother

Illuminated by black light,
my mother's life phosphoresced a sadness—

an imagined girlhood
eclipsed by her mother

pubescence wilted
by her shyness

ambition called to spoilage
by dyslexia

longings mashed down
in the blur of the thirties

fimbrial journeys unnourished
by my father

who in his dying bequeathed
her alcohol and pills.

Where are you now, coltish girl
who raised me to life?

Where will you be when molecules
vanish at the end of time?

Pittsburgh Writ Large
Notes for a fiftieth high school reunion

1.

It's a straight shot on what's now United
from Houston to Pittsburgh,
yet somehow getting ready
I feel the need for special provisions,
to bring along essentials—
like Dostoyevsky and the marvelous Gruschenka.

2.

The mills are gone, the barges
and slag heaps, the skies
a crucifying red during
and after the war. And we,
unique and sentient, look
to see who we are beyond
our jobs and health care—
what we define besides ourselves.

3.

Reunion.
These days we are gathered in,
gathered together, gathered to
the unearned nostalgia survival
allows, not sure what we bring,
not sure what we want to take away.

4.

Try to imagine concatenated lives,
or, better, lives tethered at a point
too distant to remember clearly,
impossible to reconstruct.
Desperately, though only for a moment,
we hammer the past into links
for the present, desperately,
though not too desperately.

5.

Sitting on the fault line of America,
the tectorial plates of behavior
that separate east from midwest, Pittsburgh
teetered and spilled us across the country.

6.

We have come from afar,
which is where we always were,
even if today we come
from Oakland or Point Breeze
which are as far away
from those days as Brazil or London.
But closer than these is death.

7.

I do not remember the last ball game
I saw in Pittsburgh in the fifties—
though for sure it was in Forbes Field,

but how could I forget Senta in the sixties
in the Syria Mosque saving the Dutchman
from his curse, I, buying it all,
sure that Wagner was a genius?

8.

Houston is a smudge of mold
living on the coastal plain of Texas,
the bayous devoid of flow except
in times of trouble—not like Pittsburgh,
fluvial to a fault. Who of us
has waded in the waters of Saw Mill Run?

9.

Wasabi is a custom I learned late,
all of us learned late, swaddled
as we were in the chintz
of Pittsburgh, sustained by
locally ordained Heinz mustard.

10.

Who knew growing up
C. G. Jung was a genius?
He died when we were twenty—
not even his surfaces visible
to me as I mined Freud's
Interpretation of Dreams, certain
he had mapped the known universe.

11.

Afeitar, meaning to shave in Spanish,
oddly conjures sipping tequila in Austin,
a lime between my teeth, remembering
Dutch Bill's Tijuana Bar, never imagining,
as I tossed back shots of Old Mister Boston,
a life lived south of Pittsburgh.

12.

Ike was president in 1959. I liked Ike.
Who could not like Ike?
Those were my Republican years—
wedged between hormones and want, and throbbing.
I was privileged to believe in my entitlement.
Republican like my parents and grandparents.
Ridiculous. I couldn't vote for Tricky Dick,
even before Watergate—not by the sixties.
Who could not like Ike?

13.

We are sequestered together
in molten glass or amber,
trapped in an impossible viscosity
from which we have no desire
to escape—though we must, if only
to avoid the suffocation of paradise.

Beginnings

Through one window
the Chrysler Building perches
in the south sky, in another the tops
of the trees carpet Central Park.
The apartment with its fine views
was a find, the man said.
It had been the woman's
before their midlife marriage.
Perhaps as recompense for suffering
or drifting or whatever it was
that led them to their lives alone
chance granted them this commerce
above the raggle-taggle chaos
of survival here. It's a straight shot
on the subway door to door
to my office downtown, he said.
Later I remembered my first attempt
as a boy in Pittsburgh to start seedlings
in our basement—the pale stems,
the ghostly leaves, cripples, but
implacable in their search for light.

Brazil

Brazil—not the burgeoning country of two hundred million plus and counting that Spanish speakers have their jaws around and gnaw to get a piece of, that Botero's women in Medellín grow fat on as they imagine the Amazon with its piranhas and half-discovered peoples, that Stefan Zweig thought a haven from his ghosts and for which Oscar Niemeyer, the jaguar of architects, designed a capital and a cathedral in Rio with its favelas where the poor survive on the trickle down of narcos and tourist visits, not the country hosting the Olympics, not the one that harbored Nazis and inspired "The Boys from Brazil" (or its lovely sequel "Where the Girls Are"), nor the one with so much gas it gives you indigestion just thinking about it, nor the exporter of delicious telenovelas, not the Brazil of gritty, muscular São Paulo or the one that Villa-Lobos captured, not the one with leftist politics and rightist business sense, nor the one whose argot dwarfs the pipsqueak of Portugal, not the one whose disappearing rain forests threaten to leave us breathless, as breathless as Rio's harbor leaves us, not the one with strange medicines hiding in the leaves of tropical plants waiting for the intrusive fingers of pharmacognosists to discover what the indians already know, not that one at all, not the color-blind country of the black north, the white south, and the brown jungle where everyone says color doesn't matter and it does. This Brazil—the hot coal in the mouth of South America, a molten churning core, a cauldron of plasma and hydrogen, fusion, whose only goal is heat, the Brazil that's too hot to handle and too hot not to.

Groundswell for Rain

Houston, Texas
Fall, 2011

My roses, immune to pests
and mildew, are skeletal in this drought,
their force and fragrance given out.

The ground is brown, a monk's kaftan,
so hardpan you could break a spade
to turn the earth to some good use.

In the park the pines are stripped
and cured like ship masts
that only need be ripped and trucked.

I must discard my brief for abuse,
punishment for sin or dereliction,
the idea that I can fix a blame.

It's just La Niña's frolic,
awash in the froth of the cool Pacific,
as she rides the condor swells aloft.

The gods are deaf or even feckless
perhaps malicious, maybe reckless—
yet it goes against the human grain
not to pray they kindle rain.

Remembering Two Teachers

Something should be said of Lowell Innes and Willard Mead,
a commerce of decency running between them, I, listening
on the wire—trying to understand Brutus' fault.

Poetry Review

Excerpted from the "Literature in Brief"
section of a national literary magazine

In this overlong début collection,
the poet, a returning veteran, chronicles
the campaign in Anatolia—its pathos—
and delivers a smart, snappy but ultimately
unsatisfying saga. Without giving too much away,
I can say that it has all the elements of a thriller—
a love triangle, abduction, wrath and rancor,
force, betrayal, honor and egregious disregard
for all things sacred. And catchy tropes
that are sure to make it well-remembered.
Several city-states have already bought
the auditory rights. A written version is planned.
No thought has been given to translation.
So unless you are a linguist, it will all
be Greek to you. A sequel is in the works.

Damascus Gate

Stretch Variation III
Frank Stella (1970)
MFA, Houston, Texas

The jasmine are readying themselves—
every blossom sheathed to the hilt
in a monochrome of green.

They prepare without arrogance—
their white flowers riots of modesty,
the only clue, their fragrance.

They cannot imagine "Damascus Gate"—
at my front door they sit in Moorish curls,
their tendrils do not grasp its bursting saturation.

Its prism fails the jasmine's vision, Paul's.
He was impaled on blindness by the light
as dark unraveled giving birth to sight.

Metamorphosis

You are a bubble
trapped beneath the ice,
your form distorted
to an impotent boil.
When will you have
the heat to break free,
to hiss from the cold
into the light?
Your rendezvous with me
will be meager,
evanescent only—
a brush of my lips
across your fledge
as you flare skyward,
released to a hawk-like you,
not prefigured
by the spirit level
of your dispirited entrapment.

Witness Protection Program

A poem is a witness protection program.
You change the venue and the gender,
and every personal scrap is safe.
Whatever mayhem or malfeasance
your report is hidden—you broadcast
from a yurt in Siberia (without transmitter).
Nobody can find you, but most likely no one's looking.
One hundred fifty-four sonnets later
and we don't know who the dark lady is,
what they did, and, perhaps, not even
who wrote the poems (although on this I differ).
Post something online, even on an obscure site,
and sooner or later it will be discovered.
Not a poem. If something's in a poem,
you can be sure no one reads it.
No need to encrypt bad behavior.
It's like binge drinking in a hotel room
in a foreign city or committing petty crime
in the face of terrorism, rape or murder.
No one spends the night with poems.
The few who do have secrets of their own to keep.
You can dress a pig up naked and no one notices.
And those who do, parade pigs of their own
in poems you don't read.
You can put cunnilingus in a poem (near the end)
since even the few readers who begin won't get that far,
and poets have no fear of going unreviewed in family newspapers.
Finally, people do well everyday for lack
of what is found there. There's a lot of junk in poems,
the thrashing trash of Tashkent and Tahiti.
And glorious asides—George Washington
never slept at Washington-on-the-Brazos, Texas.

After the Fall

Death blindsides you
with its lurking particulars.
You fail to notice
the macadam scraped away
on 53rd Street at the MOMA,
the raised manhole rim
that catches the toe
of your running shoe,
and you are suspended—
nowhere for an instant.
And there, without regard
to flaws or fame,
good deeds or bad behavior,
without judgment,
chance deals your hand.
Inside, on an upper floor
death sits patiently.
Otto Dix and George Grosz
catch the depravity of war
and the dark pool
beneath the streets of Weimar.
Schiele dies before
his nightmares come alive.

Hospital

One August he came each afternoon
like a squall off the Gulf to drum out
Mozart on the Steinway in the lobby—
each day the same sonata, so harsh
we longed for it to pass beyond us,
north to some place ready for his discharge.

Action Plan

A man spreads a Persian carpet in the forest,
a cheap one bought many years before in a far away city,
that seals off from him the beetles and ants.
Microvermin he calls them.
He does not call the birds anything.
He does not name the trees.
He waits for a Sufi, his personal Sufi,
as if he were a tennis partner or a neighbor.
And waits for a young woman to roll by
a trolley and offer jambalaya or tamales.
He will take nothing.
He is not sure if the Sufi will rise up or descend.
Perhaps he will materialize from a rock.
The Sufi will bring poetry. He is certain.
It rains. He imagines the Sufi praising God.
Perhaps the Sufi is one of those drops.
Praise would be a good idea, he thinks.
He will begin with the pale green lichen
on a nearby stone, work his way through
cell by cell, and move on to the stone itself.
He cannot yet praise the rain.

Defining Depression

There are rivers that must be crossed,
slit threatening particulate gold in a forbidding sun.
The far shore with its cobbled landing
offers nothing but what we leave behind.

One Fine Morning

In Assisi an earthquake
has done violence to St. Francis.
But not here where I live.
A neighbor has him safe—
sequestered in American kitsch
or is it the sincere reverence
we have for old world
artifacts, religion, our past
and can never get quite right?
This March on a nearby street
redbuds are busting out all over
and St. Francis is not.
Taken prisoner, he stands,
concretized, diminutive
in a sliver of side yard,
yellow jackets swarm him,
a stockade of sticks and string
constrain him. A loquat
threatens cannonade. There are
no birds in the redbuds.
St. Francis talks only to himself.

Journey

You row alone in a boat
on a whitecapless sea.
You imagine dolphins,
mermaids, who do not come.
You row nowhere.
The swells take you nowhere.
At times they obscure
the horizon, which fades,
appears again and fades.
Ditto the shore
with its useless quays
and white buildings.
There is no motion
save the swells,
only the fear
a vortex will
drag you down.
You rely on the spin
of the earth and a gravity
to float you free,
take you to anchor
at a mooring of deep piling.

Intelligence

Where is the wind?
Inside the leaf
whirring waiting hostage
with the chloroplasts
who beg for mercy
their task too heavy
for our wounded world.

Where is the oxygen?
Captive in the carbon dioxide
a ward waiting for release
it does not beg for mercy
it is content under house arrest
not ready for the wind
unassigned as yet
to any task relieved.

Here is a catechism
that invents itself
a codex gone over the hill
merry with what it has discovered
a binge drinker with a full bar
and no way back.

Flood Stage
for Doug Miller

A river of doubt surges through me like kudzu,
its tendrils pulling out everything corpuscular.
It is firmly rooted in the moraine of a shiftless man
who sits in the cheap seats when the philosophers speak.
Kudzu can strangle you with its certainty.
Jaguars crouch on every ledge, each a Falling Water
that preys on what I have so precariously built.
When the piranhas feed, they leave only my spleen,
a cesspool of reverence for the reticular—
a scaffold that ignores what is crushed and integral.
I draw a long breath and curse them for this.
I draw another and doubt that this is so.

Poem for the New Year
La Jolla, California

The fog slides off the sea,
deposits its drops along the strands
of a spider web, its silk roads beaded
with uncharted places searching for the sun.

Waves slip up out of the fog,
none shows its hand—card sharks
or beggars, even redeemers—
as they break over me,

breakers surging up out of the fog,
surprising themselves at landfall.
What is one to make of this mystery,
the fractals that comprise our world?

The fog hides the wind in its sleeve,
harbors this great deceiver who topples
vases from the tables, lifts the cloths.
Its decisiveness unnerves me.

At the benches by the tables the homeless
yawn into the fog, compete with the crows
as they pick through the trash.
All of us trying to imagine a future.

Meditation for the Last Night of My Life
After translating some poems of Antonio Machado

Listen, if I die tonight, don't worry.
We saw a movie, had a meal,
grumbled and stopped for groceries.
What else is there except a clarity
I could cloud over with a poem?